A taste of the....

PEAK DISTRICT

KU-270-350

Recipes

Recipes

All rights reserved.

No part of this publication may be reproduced, stored in a retrieval system or transmitted by any means (electronic, mechanical, photocopying or otherwise) without the prior permission of the publisher.

Text by Stuart Adlington. First published in 2011.
This edition published in 2011 by Myriad Books.
© Myriad Books Ltd 2011
Printed in China

Publishers Disclaimer
Whilst every effort has been made to ensure that the information contained is correct, the publisher cannot be held responsible for any errors and or omissions. Please note certain recipes may contain nuts or nut oil. The photographs in this book are for illustrative purposes only and do not represent the finished recipe. Photographs © Getty Images and Shutterstock.

A taste of....

Britain's first National Park established in 1951, The Peak District covers an area of 555 square miles, lying mainly in Northern Derbyshire, but also covering parts of Cheshire, Staffordshire, Greater Manchester and South and West Yorkshire.

An area of outstanding natural beauty, from rugged moorlands to rolling hills and dales, and lush meadows to leafy forests, It comes as no surprise that tourism plays a vital role in the economy of the region.

With bustling market towns to vibrant, exciting farmers markets brimming with beautifully fresh local produce, The Peak District offers a varied wealth and diversity of foods to keep the most passionate foodie happy and content.

The town of Bakewell, undoubtedly has one of the most famous and well renowned dishes from the region, the much loved Bakewell Pudding. Still to this day, the original recipe remains a well kept and guarded secret.

Other such local recipes from the region include the delicious gingerbread from Ashbourne, and Oatcakes from both Derbyshire and Staffordshire.

The regions other dishes also conjure up wonderfully and intriguing sounding names such as Fat Rascals to Scrunch biscuits to Fidgety and Nadgers Pie. Local farmers produce the highest quality organic meat and vegetables, whilst artisan and commercial producers offer some of the finest cheeses to be found in the country.

The open moorlands and diverse landscape are home to some of the finest game, and the lakes and rivers that are a special feature of the region are teeming with beautiful fresh water fish.

In the heart of the Peak District, nature works its patient and wonderful magic, deep in ancient limestone, rainfall from over 5000 years ago is forced up through 1500 metres of British bedrock to it's source emerging crisp and delicious, making Buxton natural mineral water one of the purest natural mineral waters to be found any anywhere in Europe.

This pure source of natural water also creates the perfect growing conditions for watercress. The region produces some of the finest quality watercress beds in the land.

DOVEDALE BLUE CHEESE, FIG AND PANCETTA TART
Serves 4

Puff Pastry tarts filled with tangy Dovedale blue cheese, sweet figs and smoked bacon. Such a delicious combination. A wonderful starter, light lunch or supper dish.

Ingredients
150g/5oz Dovedale cheese, crumbled
450g/1lb puff pastry
8 fresh figs, cut into quarters
8 slices, pancetta
olive oil
1 egg, beaten
100ml/4fl oz double cream
watercress to serve
balsamic vinegar to dress

1. Preheat the oven to 200c/400f/Gas mark 6. Roll out the puff pastry on a lightly floured surface and cut into 4 rounds about 5 inches in diameter. Score a line about 1cm/1/2inch around the edge of the pastry, then using a fork, prick the inner base of the pastry circle to stop it from rising.

2. Place the pastry circles on a baking sheet lined with greaseproof paper . Fill the centre of each circle with the crumbled Dovedale cheese, then place the figs on top.

3. Drape the slices of pancetta over the top of the figs and cheese. Season well with freshly ground black pepper and drizzle with olive oil.

DOVEDALE BLUE CHEESE, FIG and PANCETTA TART

4. Brush the edge of the pastry circles with the beaten egg and bake in the oven for 10 minutes. Remove the tarts from the oven and pour over a little cream onto each tart. Return to the oven for a further 5 minutes. Dress the watercress with a drizzle of olive oil and balsamic vinegar. Remove the tarts from the oven and place a small handful of the dressed salad leaves on top of the tarts and serve.

SAGE DERBY SOUFFLÉ
Serves 4

Don't be intimidated by the thought of making a soufflé, it's really not that difficult, give it a go and impress your friends. Just a few ingredients to make something that looks quite spectacular and tastes simply delicious.

Ingredients
110g/4oz Sage Derby cheese, grated
4 tbsps grated parmesan cheese
melted butter for greasing the mould
300ml/10fl oz milk
1 bay leaf
50g/2oz butter
50g/2oz plain flour
5 free range eggs, separated
1 tsp dijon mustard

1. Preheat the oven to 200c/400f/Gas mark 6. Brush the inside of a large souffle dish with the melted butter, then pour in the

parmesan cheese and swirl it around the inside of the dish until evenly and completely covered.

2. Shake out any excess cheese, then using your finger run it around the lip of the mould to create a neat finish, this will help the souffle rise evenly as it cooks.

3. Bring the milk to the boil in a saucepan with the bay leaf, then remove from the heat, set aside and leave to infuse.

4. Melt the butter in a heavy based saucepan until foaming, stir in the flour and cook, stirring continually for 2-3 minutes until the butter and flour have fully combined. Gradually pour in the warmed infused milk a little at a time, stirring or whisking continually until all the milk has been absorbed into the butter and flour mixture and has formed a smooth sauce free of lumps. Simmer the sauce very gently, stirring from time to time for about 5 minutes.

5. Remove from the heat, discard the bay leaf. Whisk in the egg yolks, one at a time, then stir in the mustard. Season the sauce well with salt and freshly ground black pepper. Gently stir in the grated cheese until melted and well combined.

6. Fill a large shallow baking tray one third full of boiling water and place in the oven. This will be used to cook the soufflé, as the water bath will help cook the souffle more gently and evenly.

7. In a grease free clean bowl whisk the egg whites until they form soft peaks, add a third of the beaten egg whites into the cheese mixture, this will help loosen the mixture slightly,

then gently but thoroughly fold in the remaining egg whites with a metal spoon, taking care not to beat the air out of the egg whites, but still ensuring the mixture is well combined.

8. Carefully pour the mixture into the prepared souffle mould, ensuring you clean any excess that may have spilt over the side as this will prevent the mixture rising evenly during cooking. Run your finger around the rim of the dish to create a neat finish. Sprinkle the remaining tarragon leaves over the top of the soufflé.

9. Carefully remove the water filled baking tray from the oven and place the souffle dish in the water inside the tray. Bake in the oven for 25-30 minutes or until beautifully golden brown on top and well risen.

10. The soufflé should still have a lovely wobble when the dish is moved and a beautiful golden crust on top but remain soft in the centre.

11. Remove from the oven and serve immediately with a crisp green salad.

WATERCRESS SOUP
Serves 4-6

Ingredients
250g/9oz fresh watercress
1 onion, peeled, finely chopped
1 garlic clove, peeled, crushed
olive oil
50g/2oz butter
500ml chicken stock
225g/8oz potatoes, peeled, thinly sliced
400ml milk
100ml single cream
few leaves of fresh watercress to garnish

1. Heat the butter and a drizzle of oil in a large pan and sweat the onions for 2-3 minutes until soft but not coloured. Add the garlic and fry for a further minute or two.

2. Add the potatoes and stock, season with salt and white pepper, cover with a lid and simmer for 10 minutes or until to the potatoes are tender. Add the watercress and continue to simmer for a further 2 minutes. Do not cook the watercress too long as you want to retain the bright vibrant colour.

3. Transfer the soup to a food processor or using a hand held blender, blend the soup until smooth. Adjust the seasoning if necessary. Return the soup to the pan and add all but 2 tablespoons of the cream and gently stir and warm through. Pour the soup into warmed bowls, drizzle over the remaining cream and garnish with a few leaves of fresh watercress.

SMOKED TROUT AND HORSERADISH PATE
Serves 8

A wonderfully simple, yet delicious recipe which is an excellent starter for a dinner party or light lunch as it can easily be made beforehand and kept in the fridge.

This recipe can also be adapted to use smoked mackerel which is equally as delicious.

Ingredients
450g/1lb smoked trout fillets, skin and bones removed
225g/8oz unsalted butter, softened
juice of 1 lemon
2 tbsps creamed horseradish
pinch of cayenne pepper
pinch of ground nutmeg
7 tbsps sour crème or crème fraiche
4 tbsps chopped fresh chives
watercress to serve
2 lemons, cut into wedges
1 large crusty wholemeal loaf, sliced and toasted

1. Flake half the smoked trout fillets into a large bowl or food processor, add the softened butter, horseradish, cayenne pepper, nutmeg,lemon juice and a really good twist of freshly ground black pepper. Pulse to combine all the ingredients.

2. Transfer the mixture to a large bowl and flake in remaining trout fillets, this will give the Pate a nicer contrast of textures, the smooth, combined with the larger flakes. Fold in the sour

cream or crème fraiche, add the chopped chives and season to taste, adding a little more lemon juice if desired.

3. Transfer the pate into a large bowl or divide between individual serving plates and serve with the watercress, a wedge of lemon and the freshly toasted bread or oat biscuits.

RUMP OF LAMB with SPRING ONION MASH
Serves 4

Ingredients
4 x 200g/7oz boned lamb rumps
4 anchovy fillets
200g/7oz cherry tomatoes on the vine
olive oil

RUMP OF LAMB/CONTINUED

For the mash
600g/1lb 5oz potatoes, peeled
25g/1oz butter
6 spring onions, trimmed finely chopped
5fl oz full fat milk or cream
pinch of nutmeg

1. Preheat the oven to 200c/400f/Gas mark 6. Place the potatoes in a pan of boiling salted water and cook until tender.

2. Meanwhile place an anchovy fillet inside each lamb rump, season with salt and freshly ground black pepper and secure each rump with a length of string.

3. Heat a drizzle of olive oil in a heavy based pan and brown the rumps on all sides. Add the cherry tomatoes to the pan, season with salt and freshly ground black pepper and transfer to the oven. Roast the rumps for 15 minutes for medium rare, or longer to your liking.

4. Remove the lamb from the oven, cover with a sheet of foil and set aside to rest. Place the cream or milk in a small pan and add the chopped spring onions and simmer for 1-2 minutes until the onions are slightly soft.

5. Drain the potatoes well, then return them to the pan add the butter and the softened onions and milk and mash until smooth. Season with salt and freshly ground white pepper and a pinch of nutmeg.

6. To serve, remove the string from the lamb and slice each rump into thick slices. Arrange the lamb slices on warmed plates and serve with the roasted cherry tomatoes, spring onion mash and drizzle with any roasting juices left in the pan.

BRAISED BEEF in KINDER STOUT with DUMPLINGS
Serves 6

One pot cooking at its best, tender pieces of beef braised in a rich Kinder Stout gravy infused with herbs, packed full of vegetables, topped with fluffy dumplings. The ultimate comfort food.

Ingredients
2 tbsps olive oil
25g/1oz butter
750g/1lb 10oz beef stewing steak, cut into bite sized pieces
2 tbsps plain flour
175g/6oz, baby onions, peeled
2 garlic cloves, peeled, crushed
150g/5oz celery, cut into large chunks
150g/5oz carrots, peeled,cut into large chunks
2 leeks, roughly chopped
200g/7oz swede, peeled, cut into large chunks
150ml/5fl beef stock
500ml/18fl oz Kinder stout
2 bay leaves
1 tbsp fresh thyme leaves
3 tbsps freshly chopped parsley
splash of worcestershire sauce
1 tbsp balsamic vinegar
salt & freshly ground black pepper

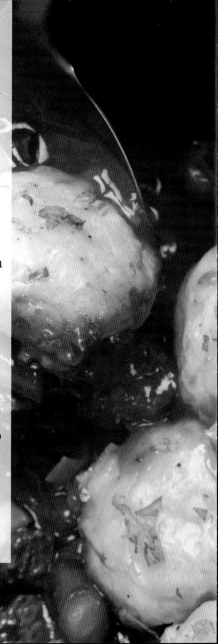

For the dumplings
110g/4oz plain flour, plus extra for dusting
1 tsp baking powder
pinch of salt
50g/2oz suet

1. Preheat the oven to 180c/350f/Gas mark 4. Heat the oil and butter in a large ovenproof casserole dish over a medium high heat until the butter is foaming, add the meat and fry until golden brown all over this will take about 2-3 minutes.

2. Do not overcrowd the pan, otherwise the beef will not colour properly, its advisable to cook the beef in small batches until all the meat is beautifully golden brown. This process will add flavour to the finished dish and seal in all the beef juices.

3. Sprinkle the flour over the meat in the pan and stir in and cook for a further 2 minutes, the flour will act as a thickening agent for the sauce.

4. Add the garlic and all the vegetables to the pan and continue frying for 1-2 minutes. Stir in the stout, beef stock, bay leaves and fresh thyme leaves, then add a splash of Worcester sauce and the balsamic vinegar. Season with a good pinch of salt and a generous twist of freshly ground black pepper.

5. Bring the casserole to a boil on the top of the stove, then cover with a tight fitting lid and place in the preheated oven for about 2 1/2 hours or until the meat is beautifully tender. Check the casserole at regular intervals during cooking and give all the ingredients a really good stir.If the sauce is too thick, simply add a little more stout to the pot.

6. Meanwhile make the dumplings, sift the flour, baking powder and salt into a bowl, stir in the suet, then gradually add a little splash of cold water to form the mixture into a firm dough. Using your hands covered in a little flour,, form the dough into small balls.

7. After 2 1/2 hours cooking, remove the casserole from the oven and place the dumplings on top of the stew. Cover with the lid and return to the oven for a further 15 minutes, remove the lid and continue to cook the stew for a further 5-10 minutes just to get a little colour on top of the dumplings. Remove from the oven, sprinkle over the chopped parsley and serve with buttery fluffy mashed potatoes to soak up all the lovely juices.

WILD BOAR PIE AND HONEY MUSTARD PARSNIPS

Serves 4-6

Ingredients
1kg/2.2lb shoulder of wild boar, cut into large pieces
olive oil for frying
175g/6oz smoked pancetta, cut into lardons
225g/8oz shallots, peeled left whole
400g/14oz carrots, peeled, roughly chopped
2 sticks celery, trimmed, roughly chopped
175g/6oz chestnut mushrooms
2 bay leaves
2 tbsps flour
200ml/7fl oz red wine
570ml/1 pint beef stock
450g/1lb ready made puff pastry
1 egg beaten

1. Heat a large casserole dish over a medium high heat, add a good drizzle of olive oil and fry the pieces of wild boar in batches until golden brown on all sides. Remove the meat from the pan and set aside.

2. Add the pancetta to the pan and fry for 2-3 minutes, add the shallots, carrots, mushrooms and celery and continue to fry for 2-3 minutes. Return the browned pieces of wild boar to the pan and sprinkle over the flour and mix in until thoroughly combined.

3. Add the wine to the pan and cook for 4-5 minutes, stirring well. Add the beef stock and bay leaves. Season with salt and lots

of freshly ground black pepper. Cover the pot with a tight fitting lid and simmer very gently for 2 hours, stirring occasionally until the boar is very tender, if the sauce is getting too thick add a touch more stock.

4. Discard the bay leaves, then transfer the pie filling to a suitably sized pie dish and set aside for 30 minutes to allow the filling to cool. Preheat the oven to 190c/375f/Gas mark 5. When the filling is cool, roll out the pastry on a lightly floured surface to a 1/4-inch thickness. Brush the edges of the pie dish with the beaten egg and lay the pie crust over the filling.

5. Crimp the edges of the pie to seal the edges, then cut a small slit in the top of the pastry to allow the steam to escape.

6. Brush the pastry with the beaten egg to create a lovely glaze and decorate the top of the pie with any excess pastry. Transfer the pie to the oven and bake for 35-40 minutes or until the pastry is golden brown and the filling is piping hot and bubbling. Serve the pie with honey and mustard roasted parsnips (see below).

HONEY AND MUSTARD ROASTED PARSNIPS
Serves 4-6

Ingredients
1kg/2.2lb parsnips, peeled and cut into thumb-width batons
2 tsps English mustard powder
2 tbsps plain flour
3 tsps clear honey
oil for frying

1. Heat oven to 220c/425f/Gas mark 7. Boil the parsnips for 2-3 minutes, drain well and let them steam dry for a few minutes. Mix the mustard powder with the flour and plenty of salt and freshly ground black pepper. Toss the parsnips in the mix, then shake off any excess.

2. In a large non stick baking tray add 2 tbsps of oil and place in the oven to heat for 5 minutes. Carefully place the parsnips into the hot oil, ensuring all the parsnips are coated in the oil. Roast for 30 minutes or until golden and crisp.

3. Drizzle the honey over the hot parsnips, give them a little shake, then scatter with flaky sea salt and serve.

FIDGETY PIE
Serves 4

A Traditional pie with a filling of apples, potatoes and onions originating from the South of Derbyshire.

Ingredients
450g/1lb shortcrust pastry
450g/1lb bacon rashers, roughly chopped
1 large bramley apple, peeled cored and sliced
3 medium sized potatoes, peeled and thinly sliced
2 onions, peeled and sliced thinly
25g/1oz sultanas, optional
few leaves of sage
chicken stock

21

1 egg, beaten for glazing

1. Preheat the oven to 180c/350f/Gas mark 4. Begin by frying the bacon pieces in a little oil until golden brown. Roll out the pastry and line an 8 inch pie dish, reserving some of the pastry to form the lid.

2. Layer half of the sliced potatoes into the base of the pastry lined pie dish, then cover with a layer of sliced onions, apples and fried bacon. Season with salt and freshly ground black pepper and a sprinkling of chopped fresh sage leaves.

3. Repeat the layering process with the remaining potatoes, apples, bacon and onions and add the sultanas if using. Pour in sufficient stock to come half way up the filling.

4. Place the pastry lid on top of the filling, trim away any excess pastry, then sealing the edges with the egg and crimping to form a neat finish. Brush the top with the beaten egg.

5. Cut a small slit in the top of the pastry lid to allow the steam to escape, then bake in the oven for about an hour or until the pastry is golden brown and the potatoes are tender. Remove from the oven and serve.

Lyme Park

Towards South Head and Mount Famine

Mow Cop Castle

SHEPHERDS PIE

Serves 6

Ingredients
2 large onions, peeled, finely chopped
4 garlic cloves, peeled, crushed
3 large carrots, peeled, finely chopped
1 kg/2.2lb minced lamb
110g/4oz mushrooms, thinly sliced
2 tbsps tomato purée
250ml chicken stock
100ml red wine
dash of Worcestershire sauce
1 tbsp fresh thyme, chopped
olive oil

For the topping
1.2kg/2lb 9oz potatoes , peeled
110g/4oz butter
salt & pepper
2 egg yolks
50g/2oz grated cheddar cheese
salt & pepper

1. Preheat the oven to 200c/400f/Gas mark 6. Heat a drizzle of olive oil in a large saucepan, fry the onions, mushrooms, garlic and carrots for 3-4 minutes until golden, remove the vegetables from the pan with a slotted spoon and set aside.

2. Add the minced lamb to the pan and fry until browned, add the thyme leaves, stirring constantly to ensures it cooks

evenly and to break up the meat. Drain off any excess oil from the meat.

3. Return the vegetables to the mince, add the tomato purée and red wine and cook until the wine has reduced by half.

4. Season with salt and freshly ground black pepper. Add the stock and a good dash of the Worcestershire sauce, and gently cook for 25-30 minutes or until the meat is cooked and the mixture has thickened.

5. Spoon the mixture into a suitable sized oven proof serving dish. Meanwhile cook the potatoes in boiling salted water until tender, drain well, cover with a lid to steam dry and reduce any excess moisture.

6. Add the butter and egg yolks and mash until smooth. Season to taste with salt and freshly ground black pepper.

7. Spoon the potatoes over the meat, sprinkle the cheese over the top and bake for 25-30 minutes or until the top is golden brown and the filling is bubbling and piping hot.

NADGERS PIE
Serves 4

A hearty pie using left over game meat topped with creamy mashed potatoes.

Ingredients
225g/8oz chopped or minced cooked game meat
25g/1oz beef dripping
1 onion, peeled, finely diced
25g/1oz plain flour
1 tomato, roughly chopped
150ml beef stock
mashed potato to cover

1. Preheat the oven to 180c/350f/Gas mark 4. Fry the chopped onions in the beef dripping over a medium heat for 2-3 minutes until the onion is soft. Stir in the flour and mix well to combine.

2. Add the chopped or minced game meat and tomato to the pan together with the beef stock and stir well. Simmer the mixture over a low heat and season with salt and freshly ground black pepper.

3. Pour the mixture into a well greased ovenproof dish. Cover the meat with the mashed potatoes which has been well mixed with butter and milk and bake for 35-40 minutes or until the potatoes are golden brown and the filling is bubbling hot.

CHESHIRE CHEESY LEEKS
Serves 4

A wonderfully simple dish, so delicious to accompany roast or grilled pork or lamb.

Ingredients
4 leeks, cleaned and trimmed, cut into 3 inch lengths
110g/4oz crumbled cheshire cheese
1 tsp English mustard
6 tbsps crème fraiche

1. Preheat oven to 200c/400f/Gas mark 6. Cook the leeks in a pan of boiling water salted water for 4-5 minutes or until just tender.

2. Drain and cool under a cold tap to stop them cooking any further, then drain again and pat dry on on kitchen paper. Arrange the leeks in a large gratin or baking dish.

3. Mix the crumbled cheese in a bowl with the mustard and crème fraiche until well combined, season with salt and freshly ground ground black pepper. Spread the sauce over the leeks, then bake for 12-15 minutes until bubbling and golden brown.

Optional: to turn this dish into a more substantial supper dish, wrap each leek with a slice of cooked smoked ham before pouring over the sauce and baking.

WINSTER WAKE CAKES

Traditional Cakes offered to hungry pilgrims attending the annual celebrations to commemorate the dedication to the village church.

Ingredients
225g/8oz plain flour
175g/6oz butter
175g/6oz caster sugar
1 egg
25g/1oz currants

1. Preheat the oven to 180c/350f/Gas mark 4. In a large bowl, rub the butter into the flour then add the sugar and currants, add sufficient beaten egg to create a stiff dough. Knead the dough lightly, then roll out on a lightly floured surface and cut into rounds with a pastry cutter.

2. Place on a baking sheet and bake for 12-15 minutes or until pale golden brown. Remove from the oven and leave to cool on a wire rack.

DERBYSHIRE OATCAKES

These traditional oatcakes can be served straight from the pan with a sweet sauce or topping, or alternatively left to cool, then fried in a little oil, served with eggs and bacon for breakfast or brunch.

Ingredients
450g/1lb fine oatmeal
450g/1lb plain flour
25g/1oz fresh yeast
1 tsp sugar
1 tsp salt
2 1/2 pints warm water

1. Begin by creaming together the fresh yeast, sugar and half a pint of the warm water. In a large bowl mix together the sifted flour, salt and oatmeal, then add the yeast mixture into the dry ingredients.

2. Gradually add the remaining warm water, stirring well with a wooden spoon to form a thin batter. Cover the batter and leave in a warm place for about half an hour or until the mixture has risen.

3. Grease a large frying pan over a medium high heat, then pour ladles of the batter into the hot pan and cook for 2-3 minutes on either side until lightly golden brown. Keep the oatcakes warm whilst you repeat the process until all the batter is used up.

THOR CAKE

A traditional cake eaten on Bonfire Night. Thor cakes were originally baked in a tin about 2 inches in depth, but this variation makes a thinner, crispier type of biscuit but still retaining the original ingredients.

Ingredients
225g/8oz medium oatmeal
225g/8oz self raising flour
225g/8z demerara sugar
1tsp baking powder
175g/6oz butter
175g/6oz black treacle
pinch of salt
pinch of mace
pinch of nutmeg
50g/2oz candied peel

1. Preheat the oven to 190c/375f/Gas mark 4. Gently warm together the butter and treacle in a small saucepan. Place all the dry ingredients together in a large bowl then add the warmed treacle and butter and mix well to combine.

2. Gently knead the mixture and roll out on a lightly floured surface and cut into thin rounds, place on a lightly greased baking sheet and bake for 10 minutes. Remove from the oven and leave to cool.

ASHBOURNE GINGERBREAD

Local legend states that traditional Ashbourne Gingerbread is made from a recipe that was acquired from French prisoners of war who were held captive in the town during the Napoleonic Wars.

Ingredients
175g/6oz self raising flour
1 tsp ground ginger
2 eggs, beaten
1/2 tsp ground nutmeg
1/2 tsp ground cinnamon
2 tbsps black treacle
75g/3oz butter, melted
150g/5oz dark muscovado sugar
85ml milk
pinch of salt

1. Preheat the oven to 180c/350f/Gas mark 4. Sieve together the flour, spices and salt into a large bowl. Beat in the eggs, milk treacle, melted butter and sugar and mix well to combine all the ingredients.

2. Pour the mixture in a well greased and lined 18cm cake or loaf tin and bake for 40-45 minutes. Remove from the oven, leave to cool slightly then remove from the tin and cool on a wire rack.

3. The gingerbread is delicious, sliced and served cold, or eaten warm with custard or cream.

PEAK DISTRICT PARKIN

Oatmeal Parkin is so delicious, but do try and make sure you leave it at least a week before eating, that way it will become beautifully moist and sticky.

Ingredients
225g/8oz self raising flour
225g/8oz medium oatmeal
110g/4oz soft brown sugar
2 tsps ground ginger
300g/11oz black treacle
75g/3oz margarine
1 egg beaten
1 tbsp milk
1 tsp bicarbonate of soda
pinch of salt

1. Preheat the oven to 140c/275f/Gas mark 1. Place the treacle, sugar and margarine in a saucepan over a low heat and stir until all the sugar has melted and the ingredients are well combined.

2. In a large bowl, add the oatmeal, flour, ginger, a pinch of salt and the bicarbonate of soda. Stir in the treacle mixture, followed by the egg and milk and stir well to thoroughly combine all the ingredients.

3. Pour the mixture into greased 20cm/8inch square cake tin and bake for 1 1/2 hours. Remove from the oven, allow to cool in the tin for 30 minutes before turning out. Store in an airtight container and leave to mature for a week if you can resist it.

BAKEWELL TART
Serves 8

For the pastry
300g/11oz plain flour, plus extra for dusting
150g/5oz butter
25g/1oz sugar
1 egg, plus extra to glaze
2 tbsps milk

For the filling
225g/8oz butter, softened
225g/8oz sugar
225g/8oz ground almonds
3 eggs
zest of 1 lemon
50g/2oz plain flour
few drops of almond extract
4-5 tbsps raspberry jam
50g/2oz flaked almonds
icing sugar to dust, optional

1. Begin by making the pastry, place the flour, butter, sugar and the egg in a food processor and pulse to combine, add a touch of milk to bring the ingredients together if necessary. The pastry can easily be made by hand also.

2. Turn the dough out onto a lightly floured surface and roll out until large enough to carefully line a 26cm/10inch loose bottomed tart tin. Line the tin with the pastry and place in the fridge to chill for an hour.

3. Preheat the oven to 200c/400f/Gas mark 6. Remove the pastry lined tart tin from the fridge, line with a sheet of greaseproof paper and fill with baking beans or rice. Bake the tart blind for 15-20 minutes.

4. Remove the paper and beans and brush the pastry with the additional beaten egg and return to the oven for 3-4 minutes, this will help seal the pastry. Remove from the oven when the pastry is lightly golden brown. Reduce the oven temperature to 180c/350f/Gas mark 4.

5. To make the filling, beat the softened butter and sugar together until pale and fluffy. Mix in the ground almonds, then beat in the eggs one at a time, beating well between each addition - don't worry if the mixture begins to split, simply add a little of the flour.

6. Fold in the remaining flour, almond extract and lemon zest. Generously spread sufficient jam over the cooked pastry tart to evenly cover the base. Evenly spread the filling mixture on top of the jam and sprinkle the top with the flaked almonds.

7. Bake in the preheated oven for 20-25 minutes or until the top is beautifully golden brown and a skewer inserted in the centre comes out clean. If the top is getting to brown, simply cover the tart with a sheet of greaseproof paper. Remove from the oven, leave to cool, dust with a little icing sugar if desired.

BAKEWELL PUDDING
Serves 4-6

Ingredients
175g/6oz sugar
110g/4oz butter, melted
5 egg yolks
1 whole egg
25g/1oz ground almonds
4 tbsps raspberry jam
110g/4oz puff pastry

1. Preheat the oven to 180c/350f/Gas mark 4. Roll out the pastry and line a suitably sized baking dish. Spread a thin layer of jam over the base of the pastry.

2. In a large bowl, beat together the eggs, sugar, melted butter and the ground almonds until well combined. Pour the filling mixture into the lined pastry dish and bake for 50-60 minutes until the filling is just set and golden brown.

MELANDRA LOAF
Makes a 900g/2lb loaf

A fruity tea loaf dedicated to the Roman Fort at Glossop.

Ingredients
600g/1lb 5oz plain flour
25g/1oz fresh yeast
1 tsp sugar
1/2 tsp salt
50g/2oz lard
210ml/7fl oz milk, blood heat
50g/2oz currants
110g/4oz fresh diced or tinned pineapples, drained
110g/4oz glacé cherries,halved
110g/4oz dates, roughly chopped
110g/4oz walnuts, chopped

1. Dissolve the fresh yeast and sugar in the warmed milk. Sieve the flour into a large bowl with the salt and rub in the lard. Pour the yeast and sugar mixture into the flour to create a dough.

2. Turn the dough out onto a lightly floured board and knead well for 5-10 minutes until the dough is smooth. Add the fruit and nuts and mix into the dough.

3. Cover the dough lightly with a clean tea towel or lightly oiled piece of clingfilm and set the dough aside in a warm place for 30 minutes.

4. Knead the dough again for 5 minutes then place into a greased 2lb loaf tin and once again set aside in a warm place for 1-1 1/2 hours until well risen.

5. Meanwhile preheat the oven to 190c/375f/Gas mark 5. Bake the loaf in the preheated oven for an hour until well risen and golden brown. Remove from the oven and allow to cool on a wire cooling rack.

FAT RASCALS

Serves 6

Ingredients
150g/5oz plain flour
150g/5oz self raising flour
1 tsp baking powder
50g/2oz lard, diced
75g/3oz butter, diced
zest of 1 orange and 1 lemon
1/2 tsp ground cinnamon
1/2 tsp ground nutmeg
50g/2oz currants
50g/2oz raisins
50g/2oz sultanas
50ml/ 1 3/4 fl oz double cream
2 eggs, beaten
50g/2oz glacé cherries, halved
50g/2oz flaked almonds

1. Preheat the oven to 200c/400f/Gas mark 6. Line a baking tray with greaseproof paper.

2. Sieve the flours, spices and the baking powder into a large bowl. Add the diced butter and lard and rub into the flour mixture using your fingertips until it resembles fine breadcrumbs.

3. Add the sugar, dried fruit and zest and mix well to combine. Stir in the cream and half the eggs until the mixture comes together to form a dough. Cut the dough into 6 pieces and shape into rounds 2cm/1inch deep and place on the baking sheet.

4. Brush the top with the remaining egg, then sprinkle over the cherries and almonds. Bake in the oven for 15-20 minutes, or until golden brown.

5. Remove from the oven and set aside to cool slightly. Serve warm with clotted cream, jam and butter.

SCRUNCH BISCUITS
Makes 12

Delicious oaty biscuits.

Ingredients
250g/8oz rolled oats
50g/2oz demerara sugar
75g/3oz butter, softened

2 tbsps golden syrup
2 drops almond extract

1. Preheat the oven to 180c/350f/Gas mark 4. In a large mixing bowl, beat the butter until it is soft and creamy, then beat in the remaining ingredients.

2. Press the mixture into a well greased shallow baking tray to about half an inch in thickness. Bake in the oven for 20-25 minutes or until the top is beautifully golden brown.

3. Remove from the oven, cut into squares whilst still hot, but leave to cool in the tin until completely cold before serving.

BONFIRE NIGHT TOFFEE

A simple yet delicious toffee recipe traditionally eaten on the 5th November.

Ingredients
450g/1lb demerara sugar
110g/4oz butter
110g/4oz treacle
1 tbsp vinegar
1 tbsp water
1 tbsp milk

1. Place all the ingredients except the vinegar into a saucepan and gently bring to a boil, continually stirring. Continue to stir and gently boil the mixture for 15-20 minutes.

2. To test to see if the toffee is ready, simply drip a small amount into a cup of cold water, the mixture should solidify and become brittle.

3. Stir the vinegar into the mixture then pour the toffee into well greased shallow baking trays. Be very careful as you pour as the mixture will be very hot.

4. When the toffee is nearly set, score deeply with a sharp knife into bite sized squares. When the toffee is complete cool, break into pieces and enjoy.